# Fall is Fabulous!

## Reader's Theatre Scripts and Extended Activities for the Primary Classroom

Written and Developed by Lisa Blau

Printed in the United States of America
Published by One From the Heart Educational Resources
14150 NE 20th Street • Suite #223
Bellevue, WA 98007

**ISBN 0-9640333-1-3**

*This book is dedicated to teachers everywhere who wish to instill in their students a love of reading. I applaud all of you.*

# Table of Contents

Dear Readers,

Welcome to the wonderful world of Reader's Theatre! In this resource book you'll find countless ideas for enhancing your entire program. Reader's Theatre is an exciting way to entice children to read....read and READ!

Reader's Theatre can be used across the curriculum. In addition, it can be shared with gifted students, Chapter 1 and Special Education students.

The beauty of Reader's Theatre is that there are no rules...you can use them any way you like to encourage more reading in your classroom. You can add costumes and scenery if you like, but it's certainly not necessary. Great costumes can be made by your students and a little creativity with paper plates, newspaper, and construction paper scraps!

*I have used the scripts and extended activities found in this resource book with my students. Much of the artwork that you see in this book was created by them...and I am both extremely proud and pleased that my students could be part of this publication. Afterall, they were my inspiration.*

*Happy Reading!*
*Lisa Blau*

# Helpful Hints

- It's easy to get started with Reader's Theatre...all you have to do is jump right in! A simple piece of poetry is the best way to get started. You'll find the poem, "An Autumn Thought" as the first script in this resource book.

- Make copies of the script so that every student has his or her own copy...if using paper is a problem, students can double-up and share scripts.

- It's important to model with children what I call, "Reader's Theatre Etiquette." As a reader, I tell students to use a loud, clear voice with LOTS of enthusiasm. Another important detail as a reader is to maintain eye contact with the audience.

- As a member of the listening audience, students should of course be quiet and attentive, but should also follow the script as the readers perform. If one of the readers does not know a word, or loses his or her place, I let the members of our audience offer assistance.

- Use a highlighter pen to mark scripts....one for each of the speaker's parts. This helps students follow along more easily.

- Use any number of pre-reading strategies with your Reader's Theatre scripts. I often ask students to read the script independently and to mark any unfamiliar words with a green crayon. These words can be listed on the board and discussed. Now you see how easily skills can be taught and reviewed by using Reader's Theatre!

- Once the script has been performed, ask each reader to give his or her script to a member of your listening audience. By rotating scripts, every student has an opportunity to be a reader and a member of the listening audience. <u>EVERYONE</u> is actively engaged!

- Finally, take your show on the road! Invite other classes in to watch your performance. Send the scripts home for homework encouraging family members to read some of the parts. I always tell my students' parents that, "Prime Time is not a special hour on T.V., it's a special time when families can share quality time together...and there's no better way to spend time together than reading and performing a Reader's Theatre Script!"

# *An Autumn Thought*

A Reader's Theatre Script
Adapted by Lisa Blau

Reader #1 Reader #2 Reader #3

Reader #1 - A leaf is a letter

Reader #2 - From a tree

Reader #3 - That is written in gold

All - Remember me!

# The Story of Johnny Appleseed

## America's Best-Loved Pioneer

A Reader's Theatre Script
Written and Developed by Lisa Blau

| | |
|---|---|
| Reader #1 | Johnny Appleseed |
| Reader #2 | Pioneer #1 |
| Reader #3 | Pioneer #2 |

| | |
|---|---|
| Reader #1 - | Good morning! Welcome to our presentation called... |
| All - | The Story of Johnny Appleseed - America's Best-Loved Pioneer. |
| Reader #2 - | Johnny Appleseed was born on September 26, 1774 in Leominster, Massachusetts. |

Johnny Appleseed - Back then I was called John Chapman. My name would change many years later when I helped pioneers by planting apple trees. Soon everyone was calling me, "Johnny Appleseed."

Reader #3 - Johnny Appleseed loved nature. He loved animals and spent much of his childhood walking through the woods near his home.

Johnny Appleseed - When I was twenty three years old, I set off for a new adventure. I began to walk across the mountains of Pennsylvania.

Reader #3 - Johnny Appleseed carried some food in a sack. His sack was also filled with appleseeds.

Reader #1 - Johnny Appleseed wore a cooking pot on his head. He walked through the forests and began to plant apple seeds.

Johnny Appleseed - I knew that someday soon the pioneers would come to Pennsylvania. They would need apple trees.

Reader #2 - Johnny walked and walked. He cleared the land and planted more apple seeds. He planted apple seeds in Pennsylvania, Ohio, and Indiana.

Reader #3 - Johnny spent his days planting apple seeds. At night he made a bed of leaves and gazed at the stars overhead.

Pioneer #1 - Johnny Appleseed loved children. He always told them stories and made them little toys.

Pioneer #2 - Johnny Appleseed helped pioneers build their homes and barns. He gave everyone he met more apple seeds. He was a very kind man indeed.

| | |
|---|---|
| Johnny Appleseed - | I was happiest when I could help others or spend time with the woodland animals. I planted apple seeds for many, many years. It made me glad to be able to help the pioneers. |
| Pioneer #1 - | Sadly, Johnny Appleseed caught a bad fever and died. No one is quite sure when. |
| Pioneer #2 - | No one will ever forget a very special man, a loving and generous man whose name was... |
| All - | Johnny Appleseed. |
| Johnny Appleseed - | The End. |

- As a pre-reading activity, write a cluster on the board with "Johnny Appleseed" written in the center circle. In each of the outer circles write the words, "when", "where", "what". After students have finished reading the script, they can refer back to the cluster and add details and information about the life and times of Johnny Appleseed. Students can then write stories about Johnny Appleseed in mini-books cut into the shape of apples. Students can take their books home to read to as many people as possible. Be sure to add the tasty apple recipe found in this unit to the last page of the mini apple books!

- READ! READ! READ! Be sure to share these excellent books with our students:

    - John Chapman
      The Man Who Was Johnny Appleseed
      by Carol Greene
      Children's Press Inc., 1991.

    - The Story of Johnny Appleseed
      by Aliki
      Prentice-Hall, 1967. (Still in print!)

    - Johnny Appleseed: A Tall Tale
      by Steven Kellogg
      Morrow Publishers, 1988.

- For P.E. you can run a rollicking relay race inspired after the book Ten Apples on Top. Each runner must race to a teammate with an apple perched atop his/her head. If the apple should fall, the runner must pick it up, prop it back up, and go, go, go!

- Two easy art projects with apples will be the perfect addition to your unit on Johnny Appleseed. Have students create a Johnny Appleseed puppet by covering a toilet tissue roll with construction paper. Don't forget to add Johnny's trademark cooking pot for a hat! (Use pieces of foil glued to tag board and cut into the shape of a cooking pot) Students can manipulate the puppets across their desks as they read the script or their apple-shaped books. Apple prints will make a lovely addition to your unit. Slice apples of various sizes across and let students dip the slices into yellow, red, or green paint. Slice one apple lengthwise to reveal a different pattern for printing.

- Cooks in the Classroom! Here's a healthy apple treat your students will all enjoy. Set up an assembly line of ingredients and mount the directions on tag board so students can read and follow along. Yum!

**Wonderful Waldorf Salad**

For each serving you will need:

- 10 chunks of chopped apple
- 5 slices of celery
- 5 golden raisins
- 5 chunks of pineapple
- 5 pieces of chopped walnut
- 1 TBSP mayonnaise

**Directions:** Count out all ingredients and place into a bowl. Stir well then eat. What a neat, sweet treat!

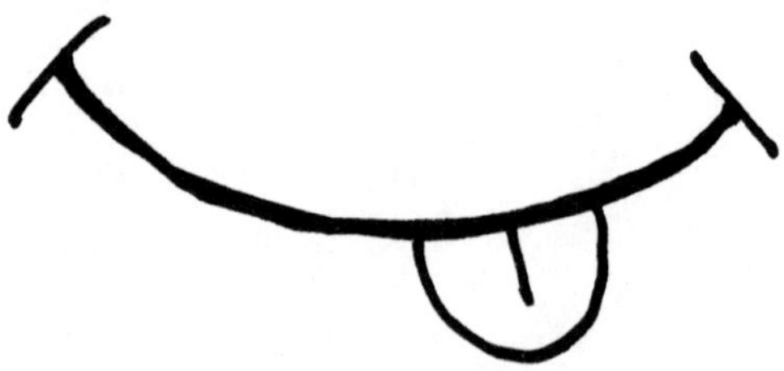

# *Across the Ocean Blue*

## *The Story of Christopher Columbus*

A Super Social Studies Script
Written by Lisa Blau

| | |
|---|---|
| Reader #1 | Reader #5 |
| Reader #2 | Columbus |
| Reader #3 | King Ferdinand |
| Reader #4 | Queen Isabella |

Reader #1 - Christopher Columbus was one of the greatest sailors and explorers of all time.

Reader #2 - Christopher Columbus was born in Genoa, Italy in 1451. As a boy he dreamed of sailing across the sea.

Reader #3 - As a young man Christopher Columbus sailed on the ocean many times. He had never sailed to the west.

Reader #4 - Many sailors of long ago were afraid

| | |
|---|---|
| | that the world was flat and that their ships would be lost at sea. |
| Reader #1 - | Sailors were afraid that if they sailed too far to the west, their ships would fall off the edge of the earth. |
| Reader #5 - | Columbus believed the world was round. He wanted to find a faster way to sail to China and Japan. |
| Reader #4 - | Columbus dreamed of the day when he could find a new way to travel to the Indies. A trip like that would cost a lot of money. |
| Reader #1 - | Then Columbus went to Spain to ask the king and queen for money. |
| Columbus - | I can sail to China and Japan and bring back many riches for you. |
| Reader #4 - | Columbus told the king and queen. |
| Queen Isabella - | I will pay for your ships. |

Reader #2 - Queen Isabella told Columbus.

King Ferdinand - We will give you money so that you can sail to the Indies. You can bring back many riches to Spain.

Reader #5 - King Ferdinand said to Columbus.

Reader #1 - On August 3, 1492, the three ships were ready to set sail.

Reader #2 - The ships were called...

King Ferdinand - The Nina, the Pinta...

Queen Isabella - And the Santa Maria.

Reader #2 - The ships were about 75 to 90 feet long. They were small and very crowded.

Reader #3 - The sailors had to eat salted meat and hard, dry biscuits each day.

Columbus - I knew that land was somewhere beyond the sea, but I had no maps or charts to tell me about this land.

Reader #1 - By now the ships had been at sea for 60 days. There was very little drinking water left.

Reader #2 - Every day the sailors became more and more frightened.

Columbus - Some of my crew wanted to return home after three weeks at sea. But I told them that we would see land soon.

Reader #2 - On October 28, 1492 the ships sailed into one of the bays of Cuba. Columbus thought that he had landed in China.

Reader #1 - After exploring the New World, Columbus sailed away. The Santa Maria crashed into some rocks and sank. Columbus was very sad. He knew it was time to return to Spain.

Reader #2 - When Columbus returned to Spain, everyone wanted to hear about his journey across the ocean.

Columbus - I gave Queen Isabella pieces of gold, fruit, and other objects from the new land.

Reader #5 - When the queen saw the gold she said...

Queen Isabella - Oh Columbus! You must sail again to the New World and bring back more gold for Spain!

Reader #4 - Columbus sailed three more times to the New World. He never found all of the gold as the queen had hoped.

Reader #1 - And Columbus never found a faster way to China...

Reader #2 - But Christopher Columbus never stopped dreaming about the lands he would discover.

All - Across the ocean blue.

Columbus - The End.

## ♥ TRIED - AND - TRUE TERRIFIC TEACHING STRATEGIES ♥

- As a pre-reading activity ask students to imagine that they are on a tiny ship in the middle of the ocean. They have no maps or charts to help them. They have little food or fresh water left. They have been away from land for over sixty days. Would they continue going further to an unknown land...or would they turn back and try to make it home? Tough choices, right?! After your discussion, tell your students that these were the very same questions that Christopher Columbus and his crew faced back in 1492. This pre-reading activity sets the stage for an exciting unit about Columbus. If you like, have students act out the roles of Columbus and a few crew members deciding whether or not they should continue on their journey or head home. Give students every opportunity to become actively involved in the learning experience.

- Have plenty of maps and globes available so that students can chart Columbus' journey either with a partner or as a member of a small group. Have students locate Italy, Portugal, and Spain as well as China and Japan. Next, have students locate Cuba on their maps or globes.

- Columbus Math! The crew members made their journey on tiny ships that measured about 75 feet long. Go out to the playground and measure out 75 feet - then let students draw a model of one of Columbus' ships. Let students experience how small and crowded the ships really were. Remind students that there were few bunks for sleeping - most sailors had to sleep on the cold, hard deck!

- After reading the script, ask students the following questions:
    - Why did Columbus ask the king and queen of Spain for money?
    - Why did few sailors sail to the west?
    - What did the sailors have to eat each day? Why didn't they bring other kinds of food?
    - Where did Columbus wish to go? Did he ever find a faster route to the Indies?
- Columbus Reading and Writing! You can add to your unit about Columbus by reading a few good books including:
    - Christopher Columbus by Piero Ventura
    - Columbus: Founder of the New World by Ronald Syme
    - Christopher Columbus by Clara Ingram Judson

- Create a classbook in the shape of one of Columbus' ships! Have students write a single fact about Columbus across the bottom of the cut-out, then have students illustrate their pages. Compile into an exciting and factual classbook!

# Sensational Spiders

A Super Science Script
Written and Developed by Lisa Blau

Spider #1
Spider #2
Spider #3
Spider #4
Spiderling
Little Miss Muffet
Daddy Long Legs

Spider #1 - Good morning! Welcome to our show called, "Sensational Spiders". You'll learn all kinds of facts about these amazing animals.

Little Miss Muffet - EEK!! HELP! HELP! There's a spider chasing me! EEK! He's going to hurt me! EEK!

Daddy Long Legs - Calm down, Miss Muffet. There's no need to be frightened of spiders. We're not all bad.

Spider #3 - 'Ole Daddy Long Legs is right Miss Muffet. Many people are afraid of spiders, but we are actually harmless. There are only a few kinds of spiders in the world with poison strong enough to hurt humans.

Little Miss Muffet - Well, I don't like creepy crawly bugs like you.

Spider #1 - Gee, I'm sorry to hear that, Muff. But just to set the record straight...we spiders are not bugs, we are arachnids.

Little Miss Muffet - Arach - what? I thought you were all yucky insects.

Spider #2 - Not so, Miss Muffet. We spiders have eight legs...insects only have six. Most insects have wings and antennae...spiders don't.

Little Miss Muffet - Too bad you guys don't have wings.

Spider #3 - Why is that Miss Muffet?

Little Miss Muffet - Well, then you could fly away and let me eat my curds and whey in peace.

Spider #4 - Say, Miss Muffet...why don't you just sit right there on your tuffet and we'll tell you all about ourselves.

Daddy Long Legs - Great idea! You'll see that spiders are pretty sensational!

Spider #2 - Daddy Long Legs is right again. There are over 30,000 kinds of spiders in the world.

Spider #1 - Spiders live in all sorts of places. They live in hot deserts, caves, mountains, jungles and even in your garden.

Spider #3 - Some spiders are as big as a dinner plate...

Little Miss Muffet - EEK!!

Spider #4 - Some spiders are as small as the head of a pin.

Spider #1 - Spiders are all predators. That means that they kill and eat other animals.

Daddy Long Legs - Most people think that all spiders weave webs...but this is not true. Some spiders hide in flowers and catch bugs there. Some spiders pounce on their prey.

Spider #4 - All spider webs are made to trap insects. A spider that weaves a web does not need to go out hunting...the spider just waits for his food to come and get caught in the web.

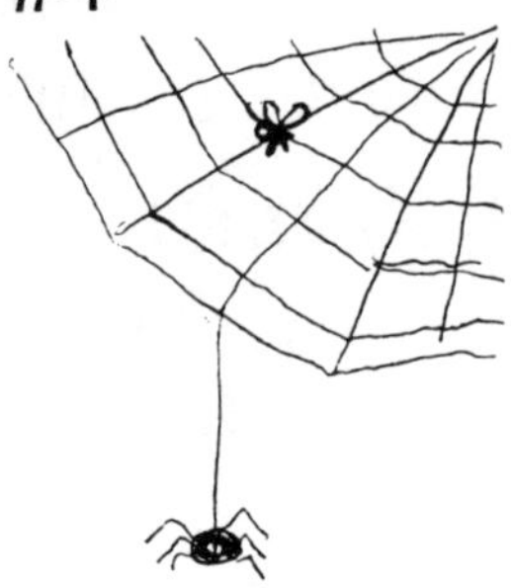

Spider #3 - Most spiders that weave webs cannot see well. They know that an insect is in their web by the vibration of the web.

Spider #2 - The spider will rush over to the insect and wrap it with silk from the web. The spider will bite the insect with its fangs. Then the spider will carry its prey off to eat...or hang the insect in the web to eat later.

| | |
|---|---|
| Daddy Long Legs - | Spiders spend much of their time catching food. They will eat all kinds of insects. They will also eat other spiders. |
| Spider #1 - | Spiders cannot chew or swallow their food. The spider sucks the liquid from its prey and leaves the hard body parts untouched. |
| Spider #2 - | Spiders lay eggs. Almost all mother spiders protect their eggs by wrapping them in silk. |
| Spider #3 - | A mother spider covers her eggs with a layer of silk. This is called an egg sac. |
| Spiderling - | Hi! I'm a baby spider! I will hatch out of my egg and then stay in the egg sac for protection. |
| Spider #1 - | Some spider mothers may lay up to 200 eggs at a time. |

**Spiderling -** Some spider mothers carry their babies on their backs until the babies are big enough to care for themselves.

**Spider #2 -** Some spider mothers do not care for their young. When the spiderlings leave the egg sac, they are on their own.

**Spiderling -** Many young spiders leave the egg sac by ballooning. The spiderling climbs to a high place and sends out a thread of silk. The spiderling holds on to the thread and gets carried away by the wind.

**Spider #3 -** But watch out! That ballooning spider may get eaten by a bird!

**Spiderling -** As the baby spiders grow, they shed their exoskeleton. This is called molting.

**Daddy Long Legs -** A spider's skeleton is on the outside of its body. It protects the soft spot of

their bodies. This skeleton does not grow as the young spider grows.

Spiderling - That's why we have to molt from time to time.

Spider #1 - Yes, spiders are sensational. They come in all kinds of sizes and they live all over the world. They even come in all kinds of colors!

Daddy Long Legs - Look for spiders in your garden or in dark corners inside your house. You might come to like these sensational animals.

Little Miss Muffet - Wow! I learned a lot about these amazing arachnids...but if you will excuse me...I need to go eat my curds and whey!

Spiderling - So long, Miss Muffet! I'll see you around!

All - And that's the end!

- A most logical...and wonderful companion to your study of spiders would be to share the classic children's book, Charlotte's Web by E.B. White. A perfect blending of science and literature!

- Go on a spider hunt! Review the script with your students...where did Daddy Long Legs tell us to look for spiders? Follow the clues given in the script and head out to look for spiders.

- Use the observation worksheet included in this unit to enhance your study.

- After returning from your spider hunt, share a book about spiders such as:

  - Amazing Spiders
    by Claudia Schnieper
    A Carolrhoda Nature Watch Book
    Carolrhoda Books, Inc.

  Review facts from the scripts and from the book. Were students able to identify parts of the spiders' body during their observations? Have students share their drawings and written observations as recorded on the observation worksheet included in this unit.

- Tasty spiders?!! Kids love these yummy treats!!! For each spider you will need: 2 "mini" chocolate covered donuts, vanilla ready-made frosting, 8 pieces of black licorice, 2 candy corns. Spread frosting on one donut, then place the second donut on top. Place legs on sides of donut. Use more frosting to secure two candy corn eyes. These tasty spiders make a perfect upper-grade buddy activity and also a nice concluding activity for this special unit.

• Super Spider Graph! Go out on the playground at recess time and ask the students..."Do you like spiders?" Use the "Playground Graph" worksheet included in this unit for students to record their findings. Many students may feel just like Miss Muffet...spiders are sensational!

• Here's another super way to integrate science and literature while presenting your unit on spiders...read Anansi the Spider by Gerald McDermott and then have students act out the story. Masks can be made from large grocery bags, newspaper, and paper plates. A blue bed sheet can become the great river...just have two children pull the sheet at each end for a rippling effect. Kids love this! Look for other stories about spiders to act out and perform for other classes. Give students exciting things to talk about and they will truly shine!

Name______________________________

## OUR PLAYGROUND GRAPH

# Do You Think Spiders Are Sensational or Scary?!

| | | |
|---|---|---|
| | | |
| | | |
| | | |
| | | |
| | | |
| | | |
| | | |
| I think Spiders are Sensational! | I think Spiders are Scary! | The only spider I like is Charlotte from the terrific book, Charlotte's Web! |

* Use your Brain Power! Write 5 sentences that tell facts about your graph on the back of this page!

Name________________________________

# Super Spider Observation Page

1.) Draw a picture of the spider in its natural habitat. Write two sentences to describe your spider.

1. ____________________________________________
2. ____________________________________________

2.) Make a sketch of a spider's web. Tell two facts that you know about spiders and their webs.

1. ____________________________________________
2. ____________________________________________

3.) Use your brain power! Draw and tell more facts about spiders on the back of this page.

I'm just BATTY over books!
STELLALUNA

# Furry Fliers... All About Bats

A Super Science Script
Written and Developed by Lisa Blau

Reader #1
Reader #2
Reader #3
Reader #4
Reader #5
Reader #6

Reader #1 - Good morning! Today we are going to tell you about a very special animal...an animal that can fly.

Reader #2 - Oh boy! We're going to learn about birds!

Reader #1 - Nope, this animal is <u>not</u> a bird.

Reader #6 - Aha! We will learn about insects!

Reader #1 - Wrong again! This animal is not an insect.

Reader #2 - It's not a bird..and it's not an insect...what kind of animal could it be?

Reader #1 - A mammal. This animal is the only mammal that can fly.

Reader #4 - Well then, it's got to be Superman!

Reader #1 - Wrong again. The only mammal that can fly is the BAT!

Reader #2 - Bats fly at night looking for food. During the day bats will sleep hanging upside-down in a cave or hollow tree.

Reader #5 - Aha! That means that bats are nocturnal. They hunt by night and sleep by day.

Reader #6 - Bats live almost everywhere in the world. There are about 950 different kinds of bats.

Reader #3 - Bats come in many shapes, colors, and sizes. The largest bats have a wing-span of 5 feet! The smallest bat has a wingspan of only 18 inches!

Reader #1 - Bats can find their way in the dark by making high-pitched noises. These noises bounce off objects and the bats use the echoes to tell about objects that might be in their way.

Reader #4 - Some bats have funny looking faces with extra skin flaps on their ears and noses. These flaps help bats make their special noises.

Reader #6 - Bats eat many different kinds of food. Most bats eat insects. Some bats eat small animals and fish. Some bats eat fruit.

Reader #2 - Just like bees, some bats feed on pollen and nectar from flowers. These bats have very long tongues. They use their long tongues to eat the nectar from deep inside flowers.

Reader #5 - Baby bats are born blind. They do not have any fur. Baby bats grow quickly. They will be grown in about two months.

Reader #4 - Bats have few enemies. The Barn Owl may catch a bat as it flies through the night. A bat's main enemy is people.

Reader #6 - People use poisons to kill bats. People destroy bat's homes. In many countries there are now laws to help protect bats.

Reader #3 - Bats are interesting creatures. We need to learn more about these furry, flying mammals in order to understand and protect them.

All - The End.

## ♥ TRIED - AND - TRUE TERRIFIC TEACHING STRATEGIES ♥

- Children are fascinated by bats. Many of your students will know all kinds of facts about these furry flying mammals. As a pre-reading activity, have students share any information that they know about bats with the class. Once you have read the scripts through several times, you can have students discuss any new facts that they have learned.

- Now that you have a captive audience of bat enthusiasts, have plenty of books and magazines on hand for students to read and enjoy. Set up a "BAT CENTER" with pictures, books, magazines, and student-created items for students to use during this unit of study. Encourage students to bring in any items they may come across from home or the public library. Students can use the accompanying worksheet entitled, "Bat Stats." Here are some of our favorite bat books:

    - <u>Amazing Bats</u>
      Eyewitness Junior Books
      by Frank Greenaway
      Alfred A. Knopf

    - <u>Discovering Bats</u>
      by Jane Mulleneux
      The Bookwright Press

    - <u>Bats</u>
      by Alice L. Hopf
      Dodd, Mead and Company

    - <u>The Little Brown Bat</u>
      by Cari R. Green and William R. Sanford
      Crestwood House

- The Bat in the Cave
  by Helen Reiley
  Garth Stevens Publishing

- The World of Bats
  by Virginia Harrison
  Garth Stevens Publishing

- Try this experiment! Bats use the process of "echolocation" in order to find their way in the dark. Blindfold students and have them pair up with a partner. Have a partner lead the blindfolded students through a maze of obstacles (move a few desks around). Have two other students act as "echo makers". These students should make noises to let your blindfolded students know when he/she is too close to an obstacle. Rotate roles so that all students get a chance to be the blindfolded "bat" and to be the partner and "echo makers". Have students discuss their experiences. What other senses did your students rely upon when they were blindfolded? Have students write about their experiences in their science journals.

- As a culminating activity, you must share Jannell Cannon's incredible book, Stellaluna. The illustrations are exquisite, the story is both tender and touching. The finest gift we can give our students is a love of literature. An outstanding book like Stellalluna will touch your students' hearts and minds and will greatly add to your study of bats.

# BAT STATS

## A Super Science Center Worksheet

Directions: You will need the following items to help you answer these questions about bats: A copy of the Readers Theatre script called, "Furry Fliers", a tape measure, a pencil, crayons and books about bats.

1.) The world's largest bat has a wingspan of ______ feet. With the help of a partner measure your wingspan (from fingertip to fingertip). Then answer these questions:

Show your work here:

My wingspan = ______________
Bat wingspan = ______________
Difference = ______________

2.) It's dinnertime! Draw pictures of three favorite bat foods. Be sure to label your drawings!

3.) There are about ______ different kinds of bats in the world. Read about two kinds of bats. Draw a picture of each bat and write two facts about each bat. You can do this on the back of this page!

Some ideas for Using the Bat Outline: Have students write stories or poems about bats. Use strips of folded construction paper, trace the bat outline onto the folds, then cut out to make a “paper-doll” style book. Kids love these!

# *Whoo! Whoo! Whoo!*
# *Let's Learn About Owls!*

A Super Science Script
Written and Developed by Lisa Blau

| Narrator #1 | Elf Owl | Snowy Owl |
|---|---|---|
| Narrator #2 | Great Horned Owl | Screech Owl |
| Narrator #3 | Pygmy Owl | |

Narrator #1 - A wise old owl sat on an oak...

Narrator #2 - The more he saw the less he spoke;

Narrator #3 - The less he spoke the more he heard;

Narrators 1,2,3 - (together) Why aren't we like that wise old bird?

Great Horned Owl - Good morning! Welcome to our presentation. We are here to tell you all about some <u>outrageous</u> birds....

All - <u>OWLS!!!</u>

Narrator #1 - Many people think that owls are very wise. This is not really true.

Narrator #2 - Long ago people thought that owls had magical powers. This is not true.

Narrator #3 - But owls are <u>very</u> interesting birds...so come along as our friends the owls tell you all about themselves.

Great Horned Owl - I am a Great Horned Owl. I am the biggest of all owls. I am a fierce hunter. I have huge orange eyes, a super sharp beak, and strong talons.

Narrator #3 - People once thought that the Great Horned Owl had horns. That's how these birds of prey got their name. The Great Horned Owl does not have horns on its head. It has tufts of feathers that look like horns.

Narrator #2 - The Great Horned Owl has few enemies, except for man and other birds of prey. The Great Horned Owl eats rabbits, mice, and other rodents. They fly silently through the night in search of food.

Great Horned Owl - I make my nest on ledges or I might even use an old nest of a hawk or an eagle. I have a deep, deep voice and when I make my call I sound like this: (low) "hoo-hoo-hoo" or "wac-wac-hoo-hoo".

Narrator #1 - Great Horned Owls also cough, hiss, or growl. These magnificent birds are found all over the world except for Australia.

Snowy Owl - Hello! I am a Snowy Owl. I live in the snowy land around the Arctic Sea. I am almost pure white. I have a great round head and wide, strong wings.

Narrator #2 - A Snowy Owl's coloring helps it to blend in with its snowy home.

Narrator #3 - Snowy Owls are excellent hunters. They eat birds, rabbits, mice and other rodents. They hunt during the day.

Snowy Owl - I make my nest on the ground.

Wolves and foxes may try to steal my eggs.

Narrator #1 - Snowy Owls stand about two feet high. They are one of the most powerful birds in the world.

Snowy Owl - I have a very deep hoot. It can be heard for miles and miles. If I want to give out a warning cry, I might whistle.

Elf Owl - I am an Elf Owl. I live in the deserts of Mexico, Arizona, and California.

Narrator #1 - Elf Owls make their homes inside a saguro cactus.

Narrator #3 - Elf Owls are clever when it comes to finding a home. They just look for a

cactus with a hole in it. They let the woodpecker make the nest, then the Elf Owls move in!

Elf Owl - I am one of the smallest owls in the world. When I am born I am no bigger than a man's thumbnail. When I am fully grown, I will be about 5 inches.

Narrator #2 - Elf Owls hunt at night. They eat crickets, grasshoppers, centipedes, and caterpillars.

Elf Owl - I may be small, but I'm a noisy little bird. My call sounds something like this "tw-jur-r-r-r."

Screech Owl - Good Morning! I am a Screech Owl. Can you guess how I got my name?

Narrator #2 - Is it because you make loud screeching noises in the night?

Screech Owl - Right you are! Screech Owls make whistling sounds too.

Narrator #1 - Screech Owls are found in the United States and Europe. They have tufts of feathers on their heads. They grow to a height of 12 inches.

Screech Owl - Screech Owls build their nests in hollow trees. Sometimes they may take over a nest deserted by other birds.

Screech Owl - During the day, I stay hidden. I am a good parent to my owlets. I bring food to my babies and watch over them until they are big enough to leave our nest.

Pygmy Owl - I am a Pygmy Owl. I am the smallest owl in the world. I only grow to be about 4 inches in height. I have a tiny round head and tiny wings.

Narrator #2 - Even though Pygmy Owls are small, they are mighty hunters. They can kill animals almost as large as themselves with their sharp beaks and strong talons.

Pygmy Owl - We eat snakes, lizards, birds, and insects. Pygmy Owls are both diurnal and nocturnal. That means we may be awake during the day or during the night. We usually hunt in the early morning or at sunset.

Narrator #3 - Pygmy Owls live in the forest or in the desert. They lay their eggs in a

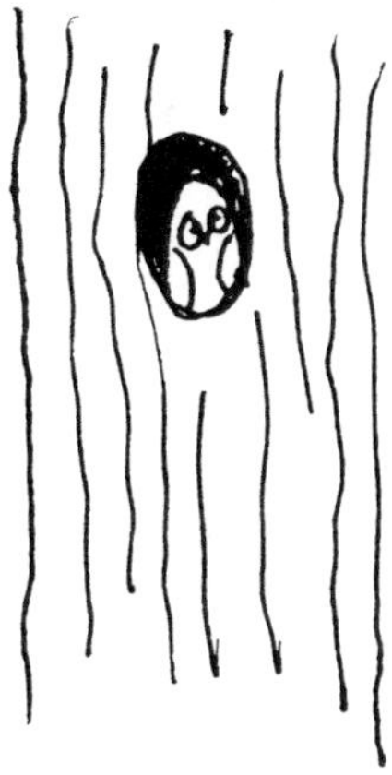

hollow tree. They may use a woodpecker's old nest.

Pygmy Owl - We have a high-pitched call, but we also make soft cooing noises.

Narrator #1 - Wow! We sure have learned a lot about owls!

Narrator #2 - Yes, we learned that most owls are nocturnal. They sleep during the day and hunt at night.

Narrator #1 - Owls hunt with their ears too. You cannot see an owl's ears because they are covered with feathers. Owls can hear the tiniest of sounds.

Narrator #3 - Owls are sometimes called "Silent Hunters" because they can fly without

making any noise. Their flight feathers are soft and have furry edges. This helps owls to swoop down without a sound and catch their prey.

Narrator #2 - Yes, owls are truly amazing birds.

All - That's right...owls are outrageous.

Elf Owl - The End Whoo! Whoo! Whoo!

## ♥ TRIED - AND - TRUE TERRIFIC TEACHING STRATEGIES ♥

- When starting any new unit, I always bring in all kinds of resources to use and share with my students. In fact, we have a special area in our classroom where we display the books, magazines, pictures, student-created items, and any other items of interest for each unit that we happen to study. By creating a focal point in your classroom and encouraging students to add to the display, you will find that students are more fully involved in each unit of study and are more interested and motivated.

- Make a list of owl-related words and discuss them before presenting the script. Ask students to define these words. Use the script's clues to help determine the meaning of any new words. You may wish to make your list owl words on a chart cut into the shape of an owl. Later, students can refer to the list when writing stories about owls.

- Review your list of owl words with your students before reading through the script. This will reinforce any new vocabulary and make for easier reading for your students. Highlight each reader's part for easier reading. Make name cards for each reader using sentence strips and colorful yarn so that each type of owl is identified. Present the script several times so that all students have an opportunity to be a reader and a listener. Tell students to listen for facts and key information as they read and as they listen. The beauty of using Reader's Theatre is that it actively engages all students.

- After reading the script, pose discussion questions to your students such as:

    - What do owls eat?
    - Why are owls called "Silent Hunters"?
    - Tell what you know about Elf Owls.
    - How did the Snowy Owl get its name?

- I like to have my students create their own discussion questions. As always, I am looking for ways to get all students actively involved in the learning process.

- Since each student has a script, divide students into groups of 5-6. Instruct students to read through the script together and to come up with questions to ask their classmates. Provide each student with a 5x8 index card. Each group member must come up with one question whose answer can be found in the script.

- The question is written on the front of the card. The answer, on the back. Students can help one another with spelling and also use both the script and your "Owl Words Chart" to help with spelling. Help students realize the many resources that they have available for their activity. Encourage students to work together as a team and to glean information and knowledge from one another. Once the cards are completed students can add colorful, detailed illustrations.

- Now for the FUN part! Each group will try to "Stump the Super Scientists" by reading their cards to the whole class. Each group stands in the front of the class. Each group member reads his card to the rest of the class. Class members attempt to answer each question. Any student who writes a question that proves to be too tough and cannot be answered, deserves a prize...a sticker, bookmark, or free homework passes are always welcomed rewards. A little certificate that bears the words, "Wise Owl Award" would surely raise any student's self-esteem.

- Once all the cards have been shared, punch a hole in the left-hand top corner of each card and attach a binder ring. Allow students a chance to read and enjoy all of the cards by placing the cards at your free-time center or send the cards home on a rotating basis.

- Make Owl mini-books. Simply xerox copies of the attached pages for your students. Read over each page and discuss possible ideas for illustrations. Encourage students to use books or magazines from your classroom display as described earlier in the packet. Once the mini-books are completed have students read them to their families and friends for homework.

- Owl Math!!! Use the last page of the mini-book to create an exciting math lesson! When students read their books to their families and friends for homework, they simply ask each person to note their favorite kind of owl. The next day, ask each student to read off the results of his/her graph. Tally the results on the board. Estimate...which group will be the largest?! The smallest?! What fun to count by fives, tally, organize data, predict, and discuss your graph! A perfect integration of science and math.

# Outrageous Owls

## A Super Science Book by

____________________________

Great Horned Owls are the largest owls in the world. They eat mice, snakes, and rabbits. The Great Horned Owl can fly without making any noise.

Elf Owls live in the desert.  They live inside a cactus. Elf Owls are very small.

---

A Snowy Owl lives in the cold, snowy Arctic.  The Snowy Owl is as white as the snow.  A Snowy Owl hunts during the day.

# Homework Graph

♥ After you read your book about owls to your family and friends, ask them to color in a square on this graph.

What's Your Favorite Kind of Owl?

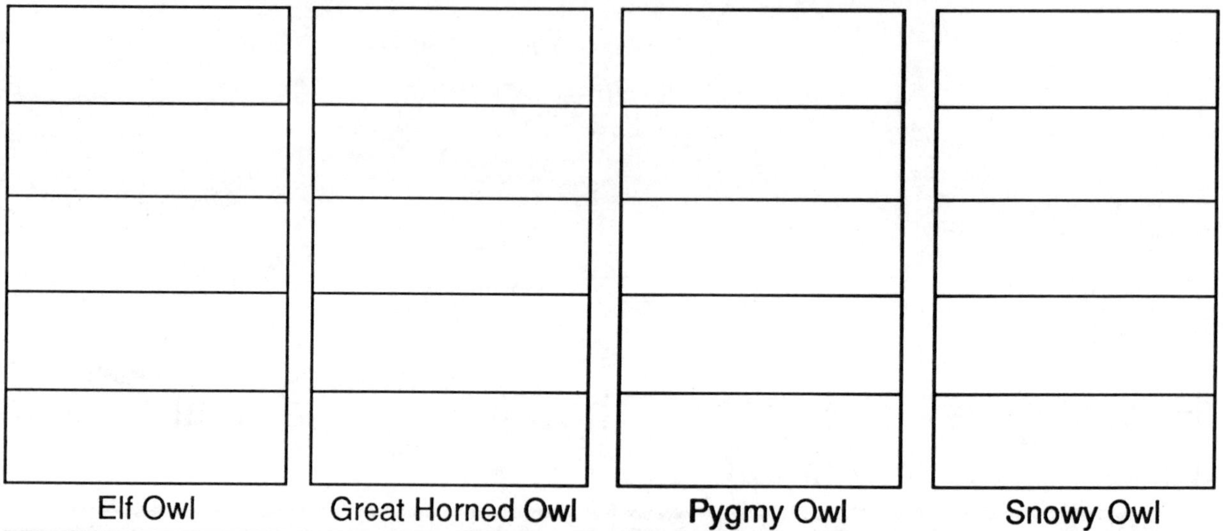


# Comments Page

♥ After reading your book about owls to your family and friends, be sure to have them sign this page with their name and comments. How many signatures can you get on your book?! Have fun, super readers!

Name | Comments

# *Farmer Fred and the World's Largest Pumpkin*

A Halloween Story

Written and Developed by Lisa Blau

Farmer Fred
Maggie May
Gus

Storyteller #1
Storyteller #2
Storyteller #3

Farmer Jones
Farmer Smith
Mayor Fuddyduddy

Storyteller #1 - Good morning! Welcome to a special Halloween story called...

Storyteller #2 - Farmer Fred and the World's Largest Pumpkin.

Storyteller #3 - Farmer Fred was mighty famous in these parts. Every year his pumpkins always won first prize at the annual Halloween pageant.

Storyteller #1 - People came from miles around just to see if Farmer Fred could grow an even larger pumpkin than last year's.

All - They were never disappointed.

Storyteller #1 - Some said Farmer Fred had a green thumb.

Storyteller #2 - Others were sure that he used magic seeds.

Storyteller #3 - Green thumb, magic seeds...who knows?! The only thing we know is that one year Farmer Fred had grown a truly remarkable pumpkin.

Gus - It was huge!

Smiley - It was colossal!

Pete - It was enormous!

Farmer Fred - Yep! People came by carloads and busloads just to come marvel at my pumpkin patch. They'd say things like...

Mayor Fuddyduddy - Amazing! Incredible! Astounding!

Storyteller #1 - Now each year the town held a pageant on Halloween Day. Mayor Fuddyduddy would look at all the pumpkins and select a winner.

Mayor Fuddyduddy - My job as pumpkin judge is <u>very</u> important. Of course, it was an easy one too. Why, you ask? Well, Farmer Fred's pumpkins were always the biggest, roundest, most beautiful pumpkins that I had ever seen. And I've seen many a beautiful pumpkin in my day.

Storyteller #3 - On Halloween morning, Farmer Fred strolled out to his pumpkin patch. It was time to pick that huge pumpkin and take it down to the pageant for judging.

| | |
|---|---|
| Storyteller #2 - | Farmer Fred leaned over and gave the colossal pumpkin a big tug. Nothing happened. The pumpkin did not budge. |
| Storyteller #1 - | So Farmer Fred called to his wife... |
| Farmer Fred - | Maggie May! Maggie May! Come help me pick up this pumpkin! |
| Storyteller #2 - | So, Maggie May and Farmer Fred pulled and tugged. They tugged and pulled. Nothing happened. The pumpkin did not budge. |
| Storyteller #3 - | Maggie May called out to the farm-hands... |
| Maggie May - | Gus! Smiley! Pete! Come help us pick up this pumpkin! |
| Storyteller #1 - | So Pete, Gus, Smiley, Maggie May, and Farmer Fred pulled and tugged. They tugged and pulled. Nothing happened. The pumpkin did not budge. |

Storyteller #2 - So Gus said...

Gus - I'll run down the road yonder and fetch Farmer Jones and farmhands Curly, Slim, and Chester. They'll be able to help us lift the pumpkin. Afterall, it's getting late. The pageant will be starting soon.

Storyteller #1 - Gus ran and asked Farmer Jones and his farmhands Curly, Slim, and Chester to help pick up the pumpkin.

Storyteller #3 - So Farmer Fred, Maggie May, Gus, Smiley, Pete, Farmer Jones, Curly, Slim, and Chester all pulled and tugged. They tugged and pulled. Nothing happened. The pumpkin did not budge. So Farmer Jones said..

Farmer Jones - I'll run down the road yonder and fetch Farmer Smith and his farmhands Scotty, Smitty, and Chance.

They'll be able to help us lift this pumpkin. They're the strongest men in this entire valley!

Maggie May - Please hurry! The pageant will be starting soon! We've got to lift this pumpkin onto the truck and get it down to the town square before Mayor Fuddyduddy begins the judging.

Storyteller #1 - Maggie May called out.

Storyteller #2 - A few minutes later, Farmer Fred, Maggie May, Gus, Smiley, Pete, Farmer Jones, Curly, Slim, Chester, Farmer Smith, Scotty, Smitty, and Chance all pulled and tugged. They tugged and pulled. Nothing happened. The pumpkin did not budge. So Farmer Smith said..

Farmer Smith - We noticed many cars and trucks headed for town. No doubt those folks are on the way to the pageant.

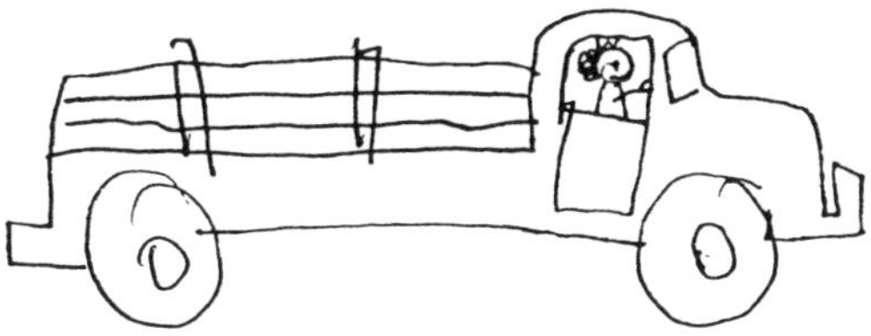

I'll just flag those cars and trucks down. We'll get enough people to help us pick up that pumpkin.

Storyteller #3 - So Farmer Smith stood out by the road and one by one he stopped the cars and trucks and asked the townspeople to help lift that pumpkin onto the truck.

Storyteller #1 - Just how many people tried to help lift that pumpkin, I couldn't say for sure. But I will tell you one thing, no one was down at the town square...they were all down at Farmer Fred's trying to help lift that pumpkin onto his truck!

Storyteller #2 - Well, there was <u>one</u> person down at the town square. Can you guess who that might have been?

Mayor Fuddyduddy - Why, it was me of course! Mayor Fuddyduddy. I was ready to begin the judging but there was only one problem.. no one was there!

| | |
|---|---|
| Storyteller #3 - | So Mayor Fuddyduddy hopped into his old jalopy. He was going to find out where everyone had gone. |
| Mayor Fuddyduddy - | Well, you can imagine my surprise when I got to Farmer Fred's house...<u>everyone</u> was trying to lift that pumpkin...but it just wouldn't budge! |
| Gus - | What should we do? What in tarnation should we do? |
| Storyteller #2 - | Gus asked the crowd. |
| Storyteller #1 - | Then Mayor Fuddyduddy said... |
| Mayor Fuddyduddy - | I've got it! Since we can't move the pumpkin, we'll have to move the pageant! We can have a picnic and hoedown right here in the pumpkin patch! |
| Storyteller #2 - | Everyone cheered and clapped. Then the party began. |

There were games like the egg toss, a pie eating contest, and even a hog calling contest. Everyone ate delicious corn-on-the-cob, sandwiches and Maggie May's famous potato salad.

Storyteller #1 - As the day wore on, everyone agreed that this Halloween pageant was the best ever. And as the sun began to dip behind the cornfields, Mayor Fuddyduddy called out...

Mayor Fuddyduddy - Ladies and Gentlemen! Boys and Girls! May I have your attention please! It gives me great pleasure to present the blue ribbon for this year's largest pumpkin to Farmer Fred. This is his biggest pumpkin ever! Let's hear it for Farmer Fred.

All - Hip Hip Hooray! Hip Hip Hooray!

Storyteller #2 - And do you know something? No one ever forgot about Farmer Fred and his huge pumpkin.

| | |
|---|---|
| Mayor Fuddyduddy - | It was amazing! It was incredible!<br>It was astounding! |
| Farmer Fred - | And this is.... |
| All - | The End! |
| Mayor Fuddyduddy - | And of course... |
| All - | Happy Halloween! |

## ♥ TRIED - AND - TRUE TERRIFIC TEACHING STRATEGIES ♥

- This is an easy Reader's Theatre script to adapt for the stage. The storytellers can stand off stage in front of the audience. The characters can act out the story. If anyone forgets a line, your storytellers can assist them, since they'll have scripts!

- Have students paint a farm scene back-drop. We included farm animals in our scenery....but with a little twist...we cut holes out for the animals' heads and had students stand behind the cut-outs. Our cows mooed and chewed cud. Our ducks, pigs, and rooster quacked, oinked, and crowed. What fun!

- Costumes are easy as pie...cowboy hats, jeans and bandanas for the boys. Aprons and western wear for the girls. If you need more speaking parts...just add more people to help come pull up the pumpkin or you may choose to use two different casts for your performances.

- Send out invitations to everyone and after the performance you can serve pumpkin cookies made by your students. What a glorious way to celebrate Halloween!

# The Story of the First Thanksgiving

A Reader's Theatre Script
Written and Developed by Lisa Blau

| | | |
|---|---|---|
| Narrator #1 | Pilgrim #1 | Squanto |
| Narrator #2 | Pilgrim #2 | |
| Narrator #3 | Pilgrim #3 | |

Narrator #1 - Good morning! We're here to tell you all about the story of the first Thanksgiving.

Pilgrim #1 - In September of 1620, a little ship called the Mayflower left England.

Pilgrim #3 - The Pilgrims boarded two ships on that day. One was the Mayflower. The other ship was called the Speedwell.

| | |
|---|---|
| Narrator #2 - | The Speedwell began taking on water. It could not make the long trip across the ocean. |
| Narrator #3 - | The Speedwell had to go back to England. Now all of the Pilgrims had to go on the Mayflower. |
| Pilgrim #2 - | Our tiny ship was <u>very</u> crowded. 102 people were on the ship. |
| Pilgrim #1 - | We sailed for 66 days. Most of us had to stay below the deck. |
| Pilgrim #3 - | It was <u>very</u> cold and damp on the ship. We ate dried beef and hard bread. We had no water for washing. |
| Narrator #2 - | At last, the tiny ship reached America. |

| | |
|---|---|
| Narrator #3 - | A search party went ashore. They found a good place for us to live. |
| Pilgrim #1 - | There was lots of fresh water and fields for planting. |
| Narrator #2 - | Winter was coming and the Pilgrims worked hard to build houses. |
| Narrator #1 - | Many of the Pilgrims got sick. There was very little food. |
| Pilgrim #2 - | It was a long, hard winter for the Pilgrims. |
| Narrator #3 - | In the spring, an Indian came to see the Pilgrims. He was very friendly. His name was Squanto. |

Squanto - I showed the Pilgrims how to plant corn the Indian way.

Pilgrim #3 - Squanto put a dead fish next to our corn seeds. Then he covered them all up. The dead fish was like fertilizer. It helped the corn grow.

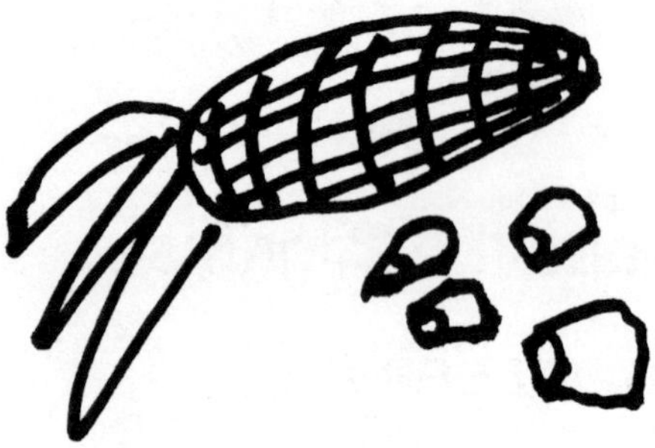

Pilgrim #3 - Squanto and his Indian friends helped the Pilgrims in many ways.

Squanto - I told my Pilgrim friends that the best time to plant corn is when the leaves of the white oak are as large as a mouse's ear. I showed the Pilgrims how to make popcorn, too!

Pilgrim #2 - The Indians taught us how to hunt and fish. They helped us plant corn, beans, and pumpkins.

Narrator #3 - The Pilgrims wanted to thank their Indian friends.

Narrator #2 - In the fall the Pilgrims had a good harvest. They had lots of food. They had homes.

Narrator #1 - The Pilgrims had much to be thankful for. They had been through hard times. They decided to have a feast.

Pilgrim #1 - We invited our Indian friends to join us. 90 Indians came to our feast.

Squanto - Chief Massasoit sent some Indians into the forest. The Indians came back with five deer.

Pilgrim #2 - There was plenty to eat.

| | |
|---|---|
| Narrator #1 - | The pilgrims and Indians ate corn bread, wild turkey, goose, and fruit. |
| Pilgrim #2 - | Our Thanksgiving Feast lasted three days. |
| Squanto - | We played many games. It was a happy time for everyone. |
| Narrator #1 - | The Pilgrims had much to be thankful for. The first Thanksgiving will never be forgotten. |
| All - | The End. |

## ♥ TRIED - AND - TRUE TERRIFIC TEACHING STRATEGIES ♥

- Ask students to imagine what the first Thanksgiving must have been like. How did the Indians and Pilgrims get their food? What were their homes like? What were their clothes like? It's important to help our students try to imagine what life was like long ago in order to gain a better understanding of history. They need to imagine a world without Nintendo and VCRs!

- In 1863, President Abraham Lincoln made Thanksgiving Day a national holiday. The children will be interested in learning that the first Thanksgiving actually took place in mid-October. November would have been too late after the harvest. We celebrate Thanksgiving on the fourth Thursday of November as established by Lincoln.

- Here are more interesting Thanksgiving facts to share with your students:

  - Cranberries were not served at the first Thanksgiving! There were cranberries growing near the Pilgrim's settlement, yet they didn't serve any at the first Thanksgiving!

  - Corn was the most valuable thing in the Pilgrim settlement. Corn was actually more valuable to the Pilgrims than silver during the first few years.

  - The tribe of Indians that befriended the Pilgrims were called the Wampanoag. Their name means, "People of the Dawn Land".

  - The Indians helped the Pilgrims in many ways. Ask your students to recall some of the ways that the Indians helped the Pilgrims as stated in the script. The Indians also:

- taught the Pilgrims how to get syrup from a maple tree
- taught the Pilgrims how to build canoes
- taught the Pilgrims how to make snow shoes
- taught the Pilgrims how to make hammocks
- gave the Pilgrims the names for such items as "raccoons" and "squash"

# *In the Days of the Pilgrims*

A Super Social Studies Script
Written by Lisa Blau

Historian
Pilgrim Mother
Pilgrim Boy
Pilgrim Girl
Pilgrim Father

Historian - Good morning! Welcome to our presentation called, "In the Days of the Pilgrims." My name is ______________ (add student's name). I will be reading the part of the Historian.

Pilgrim Mother - Good Day. My name is ______________ (add student's name). I will be reading the part of the Pilgrim Mother.

Pilgrim Father - Hello. My name is ______________ (add student's name). I will be reading the part of the Pilgrim Father.

Pilgrim Boy - My name is ________________. I will be
(add student's name)
reading the part of the Pilgrim Boy.

Pilgrim Girl - My name is ________________. I will be
(add student's name)
reading the part of the Pilgrim Girl.

Historian - Let us begin. Imagine if you will what life was like for the 102 passengers who set sail for America on the Mayflower.

Pilgrim Father - The year was 1620. Our tiny ship, the Mayflower was very crowded. The Mayflower carried about 30 crew members. There were 34 children aboard the Mayflower when we set sail for the New World.

Pilgrim Boy - We had to sleep on the cold, hard floor of the ship. There was little light and no fresh air.

There were terrible storms that tossed our ship across the ocean. Many people became sick.

Pilgrim Girl - We ate salted beef, pork, and fish. We ate hard, dry biscuits. We called our biscuits, "hard tack" because they were so hard and tough.

Pilgrim Mother - We usually ate our food cold. All of the stormy weather made it dangerous to light a fire for cooking on the ship.

Historian - It was a glorious day indeed when the Pilgrims spotted land on November 9, 1620.

Pilgrim Boy - Most Pilgrims remained on the ship for about four months. We had to wait for our houses to be built.

Pilgrim Father - We did not live in log cabins. Our houses were very small. Our windows were covered with cloth because we didn't have any glass. Our homes had thatched roofs made of straw.

Pilgrim Girl - Once our houses were finished, we still had to sleep on the floor until our beds could be made. Some mattresses were made of straw.

Pilgrim Mother - Some mattresses were made of goose feathers. We also used pine needles or corn husks. My children helped stuff the mattresses. This was one of their favorite chores.

Historian - Pilgrim homes had very little furniture. Can you guess why? The Pilgrims' houses were too small to hold much furniture.

The Pilgrims were so busy tending crops and gathering food that they had little time left for making furniture.

Pilgrim Father - Most of our homes had only one chair. This chair was for the father to sit in.

Pilgrim Girl - Pilgrim children had to eat their meals standing up. We could not speak during a meal unless a parent spoke to us first.

Pilgrim Boy - Our homes had no bathrooms, no electricity, or running water. In order to take a bath, we had to first fetch the water, boil the water, then stand in a tub. Does this sound like much fun to you?!

| | |
|---|---|
| Pilgrim Father - | Our children had many chores. Young girls helped grind the wheat or corn to make bread. The boys helped their fathers plant crops and tend to the animals. |
| Historian - | The Pilgrims were very brave. They faced many hardships. They worked hard every day to build a better life for themselves and their children. |
| Pilgrim Boy - | As you sit down for your Thanksgiving dinner, take a moment to remember the Pilgrims and of course... |
| All - | Have a happy Thanksgiving! |
| Pilgrim Boy - | The End. |

- Have students brainstorm a list of questions about the Pilgrims prior to reading the script. Post questions on the board, chart paper, or on the overhead. Some sample questions might include:
  - How many Pilgrims sailed on the Mayflower?
  - How did the Pilgrims cook their food?
  - How long did the Pilgrims sail on the Mayflower?
  - What kind of houses did the Pilgrims live in?
  - What kind of clothes did the Pilgrims wear?

  After reading the script, ask students to refer back to their list of questions. Encourage students to answer as many questions as they can...a second reading of the script with a new set of readers may be needed! If students cannot answer all of their questions, encourage them to do some additional research. Students could work in cooperative groups to answer the questions <u>OR</u> perhaps students could interview 5th grade students who are learning about American history. The buddy activity provides an opportunity for your students to recognize that everyone can be a teacher and a student at the same time. Your "research teams" might benefit from reading these excellent books:

• <u>Colonial American Crafts - The Home</u>
by Judith Hoffman Corwin
Franklin Watts Publishers
*This series includes - The Home, The Village and The School

• <u>The Pilgrims of Plimoth</u>
by Maurice Sewell
Atheneum

• <u>Three Young Pilgrims</u>
by Cheryl Harness
Bradbury Press

- Cooks in the Classroom!

Early Americans loved bread, but they didn't have any white flour when they first arrived in the New World. The Indians taught the Pilgrims how to grind corn into cornmeal. Afterall, the Indians had been grinding corn for cornmeal for hundreds of years before the Pilgrims arrived! The Indians taught the Pilgrims how to make bread from the cornmeal. Grinding the corn was hard work. Sometimes the Pilgrims used a hollowed out tree trunk and a heavy wooden club to make the cornmeal. The cornbread was sometimes called "Journeycake" because it could travel well. In later years the name "Journeycake" became "johnnycake". The Pilgrims tried to improve the flavor of the journeycake by adding salt, sugar, or butter. Why not try this recipe with your students as a tasty culminating activity?!

**Journey Cake**

1 c. cornmeal
1 c. flour
1/2 teas. salt
1/2 teas. soda
2 eggs beaten
2 TBS. molasses
2 C. milk
oil to grease baking dish

Mix the first four ingredients well, then slowly add the remaining ingredients. Pour mixture into an 8-inch baking pan that has been well greased with cooking oil. Bake at 350° for twenty minutes. Journey Cake tastes best served warm with butter, jam or honey.

• Super Science!

The Pilgrim Girl told us that the Pilgrims ate salted meat, pork, and fish as they sailed to America. Ask your students why the Pilgrims ate the heavily salted meats. To demonstrate the use of salt in keeping meat fresh, try this super science experiment with your students. Note: This is an excellent science activity to send home so that your students can do the experiment with their families. Easy hands-on science experiments can be very effective when they are sent home as a family learning activity.

## SUPER SCIENCE EXPERIMENT

Question: Why did the Pilgrims use salt to keep their meat fresh?

Materials That You Will Need:

1/4 pound raw hamburger meat
1 container of salt

Divide the meat into two equal portions. Heavily salt one portion of meat - leave the other portion plain. Place the meat on paper plates and leave out for several days. Observe and record the changes in both portions each day. How does the meat look? How does it smell? Can you think of other resources we have today to keep our food fresh that the Pilgrims did not have?

Here's Why it Works:

The salt acted as a preservative to keep the meat fresher. But as you probably saw, without refrigeration, both portions of meat became dark and bad-smelling within a short while. The Pilgrims cooked and salted their meat heavily to keep it fresh for the long voyage across the sea. Why not do some research...when was the refrigerator invented? What other ways did the people of long ago keep their food fresh? Have fun, super scientists!

"Wow,
did you know the Pilgrims
used salt to keep their
meat fresh?"

# READING

## ACHIEVEMENT AWARD

## Congratulations, Super Reader!

________________________________________

has read and performed a Reader's Theatre Script on

__________________________________.

Signed,________________________ Date:_________

notes

# ABOUT LISA BLAU, M.A.

**WHAT EDUCATORS SAY...**

- "Your workshop evaluations were **outstanding**. We want you back. On a scale of 1 to 5, you are a 5 !!"
  *-Dr. Arlene Sukraw*
  *Staff Development Director*
  *North Platte, Nebraska*

- It is my pleasure to "sing the praises" of Lisa Blau. Her practical and motivating strategies and ideas were presented in a manner that both veteran as well as beginning teachers found **inspirational**. We all left with a renewed commitment to enriching our students' lives through fun and educationally appropriate activities.
  *-SueAnn Smith*
  *Director of Special Services*
  *Vernon Hills, Illinois*

- The information that Lisa shared with our teachers was ready to be taken back to the classroom immediately and applied in a meaningful way with students. I **highly recommend** Lisa Blau.
  *-Janet Eubank*
  *Language Arts Teaching Specialist*
  *Wichita, Kansas*

- Lisa is a motivator. Lisa is creative. Lisa likes doing what she does and you know that fact instantly. Lisa loves people, especially kids. Lisa brings out the best in students, and tosses the rest away. Lisa teaches with a passion for learning that soon scorches the very soul of the learner. Lisa, indeed; personifies a "lust for life". If Lisa Blau wants a job, "You would be a fool not to give it to her". She is one of the best, and always gives a whole lot more than she is ever compensated. Lisa brings real joy to learning and to just associating with her. I count Lisa as a trusted and valued associate, and accomplished educator, and a true friend to kids everywhere.
  *-R.H. Iannone, Ed.D., Principal*
  *Covina Elementary School*
  *Covina, California*

**EDUCATIONAL BACKGROUND...**

Educator-consultant Lisa Blau has an extensive background in the field of education. As a classroom teacher, Mrs. Blau has worked in the Gifted Program and has also served as a Chapter I Resource Specialist. Her wealth of knowledge regarding whole language philosophy and instruction led to a five year position as a Mentor Teacher. While serving in this position, she trained K-6 teachers on the use of literature-based instruction and whole language strategies and methods.

Mrs. Blau currently makes presentations for teachers across the United States and Canada. While combining educational research and theory, Mrs. Blau provides teachers with strategies and ideas that focus on some of today's most pressing issues including assessment and multicultural education. A frequent featured speaker at conferences across the United States, Mrs. Blau has received high marks from her audiences at the following conferences:

- National Science Teachers
- International Reading Association
- California Reading Association
- South-West Regional Self-Esteem
- Washington Reading Association
- Oregon Reading Association
- Idaho Reading Association

She is a recipient of the "Celebrate Literacy" Award given through the IRA for her outstanding contributions to the promotion of literacy.

Mrs. Blau is the author of several Reader's Theatre resource books featuring scripts and extended activities designed to help children discover the joy of reading. An avid reader, Mrs. Blau is happiest when she can read to her children Daniel and Kayla.

# notes